AMAZING NATIONAL PARKS

GREAT SMOKY MOUNTAINS National Park

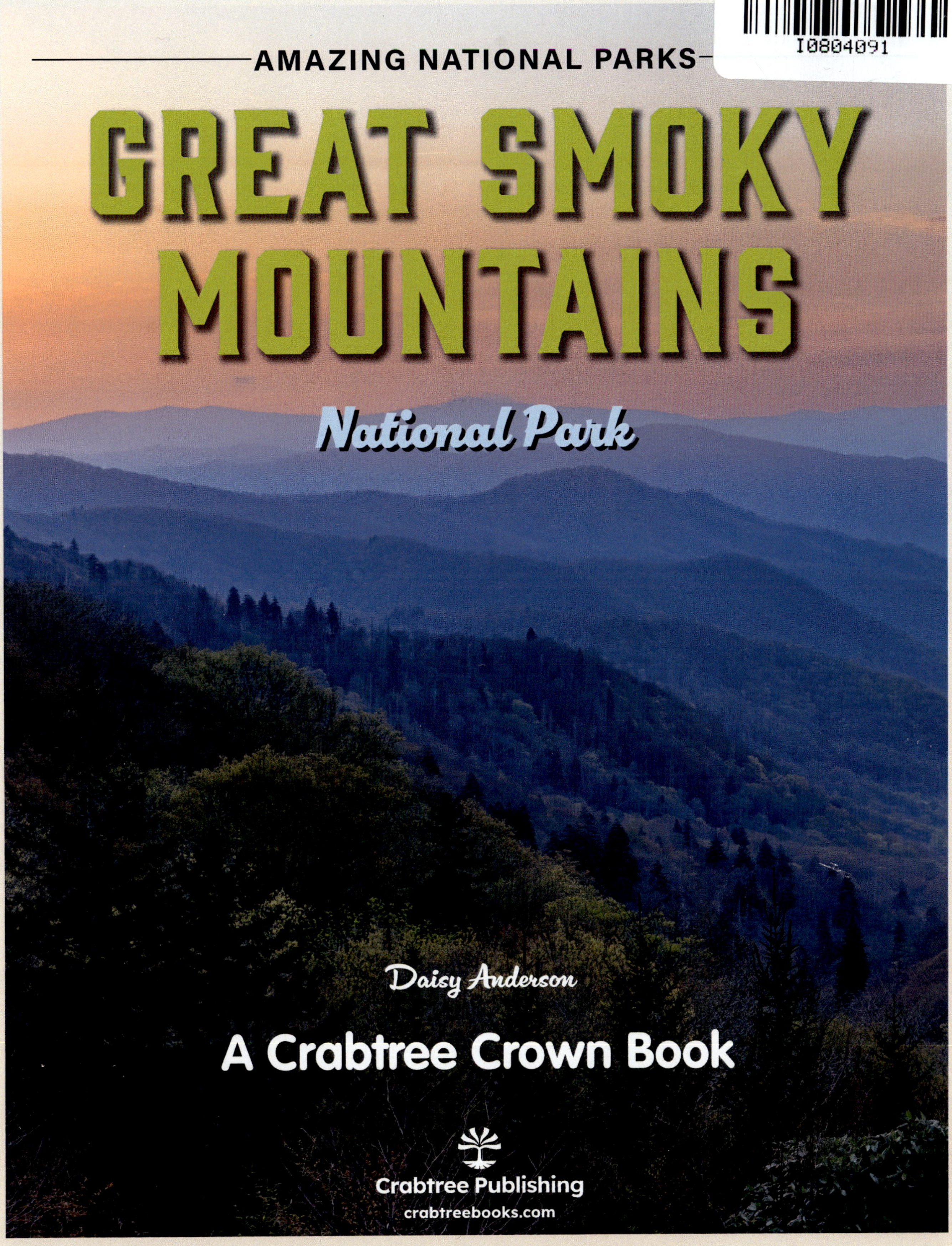

Daisy Anderson

A Crabtree Crown Book

Crabtree Publishing
crabtreebooks.com

School-to-Home Support for Caregivers and Teachers

This appealing book is designed to teach students about core subject areas. Students will build upon what they already know about the subject, and engage in topics that they want to learn more about. Here are a few guiding questions to help readers build their comprehension skills. Possible answers appear here in red.

Before Reading:

What do I know about Great Smoky Mountains National Park?

- *I know the national park is in the mountains.*
- *I know many people visit Great Smoky Mountains National Park.*

What do I want to learn about this topic?

- *I want to learn what people can see in the national park.*
- *I want to learn what people can do in the national park.*

During Reading:

I'm curious to know...

- *I'm curious to know what kinds of animals live in the national park.*
- *I'm curious to know what kinds of plants grow in the national park.*

How is this like something I already know?

- *I know bears live in mountains.*
- *I know trees grow on mountains.*

After Reading:

What was the author trying to teach me?

- *The author was trying to teach me about why so many people visit Great Smoky Mountains National Park.*
- *The author was trying to teach me what visitors can see at the national park.*

How did the photographs and captions help me understand more?

- *The photographs helped me picture what the national park looks like.*
- *The captions gave me extra information about what there is to see at the national park.*

TABLE OF CONTENTS

Chapter 1

WELCOME TO GREAT SMOKY MOUNTAINS NATIONAL PARK

Fog drifts among green trees high in the mountains. The Cherokee people named this area Shaconage—"place of the blue smoke." These misty mountains are home to the most visited national park in the United States!

Know the Park

The U.S. government owns national parks and takes care of them. National parks are used to help protect natural areas.

Know the Park

The Great Smoky Mountains get their name from the fog that hovers above the trees. The fog forms from a gas that is given off by millions of plants.

The national park covers 816 square miles (2,113 square kilometers) of the Great Smoky Mountains. This mountain range sits between North Carolina and Tennessee. The Great Smoky Mountains are a small part of the Appalachian Mountains. The Appalachians are one of the oldest mountain ranges on Earth.

BEFORE IT WAS A PARK

The Cherokee people lived in the mountains for thousands of years. They built hunting camps and other settlements there. **Settlers** from Europe moved to the area in the late 1700s. They forced the Cherokee to give up their land and leave.

Logging companies owned many of the mountain forests by the 1900s. They cut down trees for their wood. People who lived in North Carolina and Tennessee worried about the forests. They wanted to **preserve** them. They gave talks and wrote letters to the government about why they wanted a national park.

FOUNDING THE PARK

President Calvin Coolidge signed the bill to establish Great Smoky Mountains National Park in 1926. Tennessee and North Carolina gave land to make the national park. More was bought from people who owned land in the area. The park opened for the first time in September of 1940.

Anne Davis

Know the Park

Anne Davis is called the "Mother of the Park" because Great Smoky Mountains National Park was her idea. She was elected to the Tennessee government in 1925 and backed the bill to create the park.

THE PARK TODAY

Great Smoky Mountains National Park is the 19th-largest national park in the United States. It has more than 2,000 places to camp and picnic. Between 12 to 14 million people enjoy Great Smoky Mountains National Park every year!

Chapter 2

THE LAND AND CLIMATE

The oldest rocks in the area formed more than one billion years ago. The Great Smoky Mountains were created about 300 million years ago when two **tectonic plates** pushed together. The pushing plates **uplifted** the rock into mountains.

The Great Smoky Mountains may once have been some of the tallest mountains on Earth. But wind, rain, ice, and snow wore them down over time. This weathering also carved mountain valleys. It helped create many waterfalls. The same weathering continues to wear down the mountains today.

Scientists think the mountains are now eroding about 2 inches (5 centimeters) every 1,000 years.

CLIMATE

The area is **temperate** and rainy. The national park may see up to 85 inches (216 centimeters) of rain nearly every year. Great Smoky Mountain National Park is one of the wettest places in the United States.

July is usually the wettest month in the national park.

Temperatures in the national park depend on the **elevation**. It's colder at the top of a mountain than at the bottom. It might be 40 °F (4 °C) at a mountain top but 60 °F (16 °C) in the lowlands at the same time. Summers are hot and often rainy. Winters are mild, but snow falls on the mountain tops.

Chapter 3
PLANTS IN THE PARK

The national park has five forest types. Spruce-fir forests top the highest elevations. Northern hardwood forests grow in the middle to upper parts of the mountains. Sugar maples, yellow birch, and American beech trees are northern hardwoods. They are known for their beautiful fall colors.

Know the Park

Fall colors of leaves in the national park begin in mid-September and last to early November. The fall colors begin in the higher parts of the mountains and move down to the lowlands as the leaves change.

Every year, more than one million people go to see the fall colors in the national park.

Know the Park

Want to see all five types of Great Smoky Mountains forests at the same time? Visit the Carlos C. Campbell Overlook in the national park.

Pine-oak forests are found along drier **ridges**. Cove hardwoods such as red maples and dogwoods cover the valleys. Hemlock forests grow along rivers and streams.

Know the Park

The national park has forests, but it also has lowlands, meadows, and wetlands.

FLOWERING PLANTS

More than 1,600 **species** of flowering plants color the national park. That includes 36 different kinds of orchids. There are so many flowers that it's sometimes nicknamed "Wildflower National Park."

Blooming shrubs called rhododendrons cover the mountains. Rosebay rhododendrons are the most common. They burst into white blooms in June and July. Purple Catawba rhododendrons flower in the mountains' highest parts in June.

Catawba rhododendrons only grow at elevations higher than 3,500 feet (1,067 meters).

Chapter 4
ANIMALS IN THE PARK

Great Smoky Mountains National Park is full of wildlife. White-tailed deer, raccoons, and squirrels make their homes in the forests. More than 200 kinds of birds live there, too.

About 500 wild turkeys live in the national park.

Know the Park

Elk disappeared from the area because people hunted them too much. The National Park Service brought 52 elk into the national park in the early 2000s. Today around 200 elk live there.

BLACK BEARS

The black bear is the national park's **symbol**. About 1,500 live there. Male black bears may weigh up to 250 pounds (113 kilograms) in the summer. They pack on extra weight before **hibernation** and may reach as much as 600 pounds (272 kilograms). Black bears eat berries, nuts, insects, and fish.

Know the Park

It's important that national park visitors do not feed the bears. Our food is not good for them. Bears may also harm people who come too close.

Red-cheeked salamanders live under moss, rocks, and logs in cool, damp forests at elevations above 2,500 feet (762 meters).

SALAMANDERS

The Great Smoky Mountains are known as the salamander capital of the world. That's because 30 species are found there. The red-cheeked salamander is found nowhere else in the world.

WATCHING WILDLIFE

It can be hard to spot wildlife in the national park because of its thick forests. Using a pair of binoculars may help. Keeping quiet helps, too. But it's important to remember that all the animals are wild, and you should give them plenty of space.

Chapter 5

TIPS ON WHAT TO SEE

Know the Park

Clingmans Dome is the highest point in Tennessee. It's also the third-highest mountain east of the Mississippi River.

CLINGMANS DOME

Clingmans Dome is the highest point in Great Smoky Mountains National Park. It's 6,643 feet (2,025 meters) high! A viewing tower at the top lets visitors see more than 100 miles (160 kilometers) away on clear days.

WATERFALLS

The national park has more than 100 waterfalls. Some, like The Sinks, can be seen from the road. Trails lead visitors to many others, such as Rainbow Falls and Laurel Falls. More than 200,000 visitors hike the trails to the waterfalls every year.

Know the Park

Ramsey Cascades is one of the national park's most popular waterfalls. It's 100 feet (30 meters) high and the tallest waterfall in the Great Smoky Mountains.

CADES COVE

Cades Cove is a large valley in the national park. An 11-mile (18-kilometer) road loops around the cove. Visitors often spot deer, bears, turkeys, and other animals in Cades Cove. Hiking trails also go through the valley, including one that is wheelchair friendly.

FIREFLIES

At least 19 kinds of fireflies live in the national park. One kind brings people to the park from around the world. These fireflies flash their yellow lights in the same pattern, at the same time. Watching these fireflies is so popular that visitors must sign up to come see them.

Male fireflies flash their lights to attract mates.

Chapter 6
TIPS ON WHAT TO DO

Know the Park

Visitors to the national park should follow the Leave No Trace Principles. They include staying on trails, leaving no trash behind, and treating wildlife with respect.

HIKING

Great Smoky Mountains National Park has 848 miles (1,365 kilometers) of hiking trails. Some are long and difficult—one covers more than 71 miles (114 kilometers). Others are less than 4 miles (6 kilometers) and easy to hike. The national park even has kid-friendly hikes.

FISHING

About 2,900 miles (4,667 kilometers) of rivers and streams flow through the national park. Fishing is allowed in all of them all year long. Fishers catch trout and bass in these waters. Some streams hold thousands of rainbow trout.

CAMPING

The national park has camping areas for everyone. Some may be reached by car. Backcountry campgrounds are for hikers. The national park even has camps for horseback riders.

The national park's campgrounds fill up quickly and reservations are needed.

Whether you hike, camp, or just drive in for the day, Great Smoky Mountains National Park has so much to see and do!

GLOSSARY

elevation (el-uh-VAY-shun): The height of a place above sea level

eroding (ih-ROAD-ing): Wearing away over time by water and wind

hibernation (hye-bur-NAY-shun): A deep sleep-like state that some animals go into to survive the winter

preserve (pri-ZURV): To protect something so that it stays in its original state

ridges (RIH-jiz): Long areas of land on top of mountains or hills

settlers (SET-lers): People who move to a new place and make it their home

species (SPEE-seez): A group of animals or plants that are similar and can reproduce with one another

symbol (SIM-buhl): An object or a design that stands for something else

tectonic plates (tek-TAA-nuhk playts): The flat, rocky pieces that make up Earth's outer crust

temperate (TEM-pr-it): Having temperatures that are neither very hot nor very cold

uplift (UHP-lift): An increase in the vertical elevation of Earth's surface as a result of natural causes

INDEX

COMPREHENSION QUESTIONS

1. Great Smoky Mountains National Park is part of the ____ Mountains.
   a. Appalachian
   b. Rocky
   c. Sierra Nevada
2. How many types of forests does Great Smoky Mountains National Park have?
   a. Six
   b. Five
   c. Four
3. The highest point in Great Smoky Mountains National Park is ____.
   a. Cades Cove
   b. Clingmans Dome
   c. Rainbow Falls
4. True or False: Great Smoky Mountains National Park is in North Carolina and Tennessee.
5. True or False: Grizzly bears live in Great Smoky Mountains National Park.

Answers: 1. A, 2. B, 3. B, 4. True, 5. False

ABOUT THE AUTHOR

Daisy Anderson loves to write real-life books for curious kids. She lives in the Midwest, where she enjoys exploring the great outdoors with her two dogs. When Daisy isn't writing, she's out hiking and having fun in nature.

Written by: Daisy Anderson
Designed by: Bobbie Houser
Series Development: James Earley
Proofreader: Melissa Boyce
Educational Consultant: Marie Lemke M.Ed.
Printed in the U.S.A./CP2025

Photographs:
t = Top, c = Center, b = Bottom, l = Left, r = Right
Alamy: piemags/DCM: p. 6; Zoonar/alex grichenko: p. 15
National Park Service: p. 7-8
Shutterstock: Ben McMurtray: cover, p. 1; Artiom Photo: p. 4; Kelly vanDellen: p. 5 t; Rainer Lesniewski: p. 5 b; Margaret. Wiktor: p. 9; Donna Bollenbach: p. 10-11; Alexander Narraina: p. 12; Yiwenz: p. 13; OFFFSTOCK: p. 14; KLiK Photography: p. 16; Kelly vanDellen: p. 17, 21, 23; David Turko: p. 18 t; jo Crebbin: p. 18 b; Ben McMurtray: p. 19; Gabbie Berry: p. 20; Theron Stripling III: p. 22; Dean Fikar: p. 24; Elgin Akin: p. 25; Billy McDonald: p. 26; Geir Olav Lyngfjell: p. 27; Wildnerdpix: p. 28; gary718: p. 29

Crabtree Publishing

crabtreebooks.com 800-387-7650

Printed in Canada/012025/CP20250101

Published in Canada
Crabtree Publishing
616 Welland Ave.
St. Catharines, Ontario
L2M 5V6

Published in the United States
Crabtree Publishing
347 Fifth Ave
Suite 1402-145
New York, NY 10016

Library and Archives Canada Cataloguing in Publication
Available at Library and Archives Canada

Library of Congress Cataloging-in-Publication Data
Available at the Library of Congress

Hardcover: 978-1-0398-6484-9
Paperback: 978-1-0398-6553-2
Ebook (pdf): 978-1-0398-6622-5
Epub: 978-1-0398-6691-1